This book belongs to......

# Small preview of what's inside

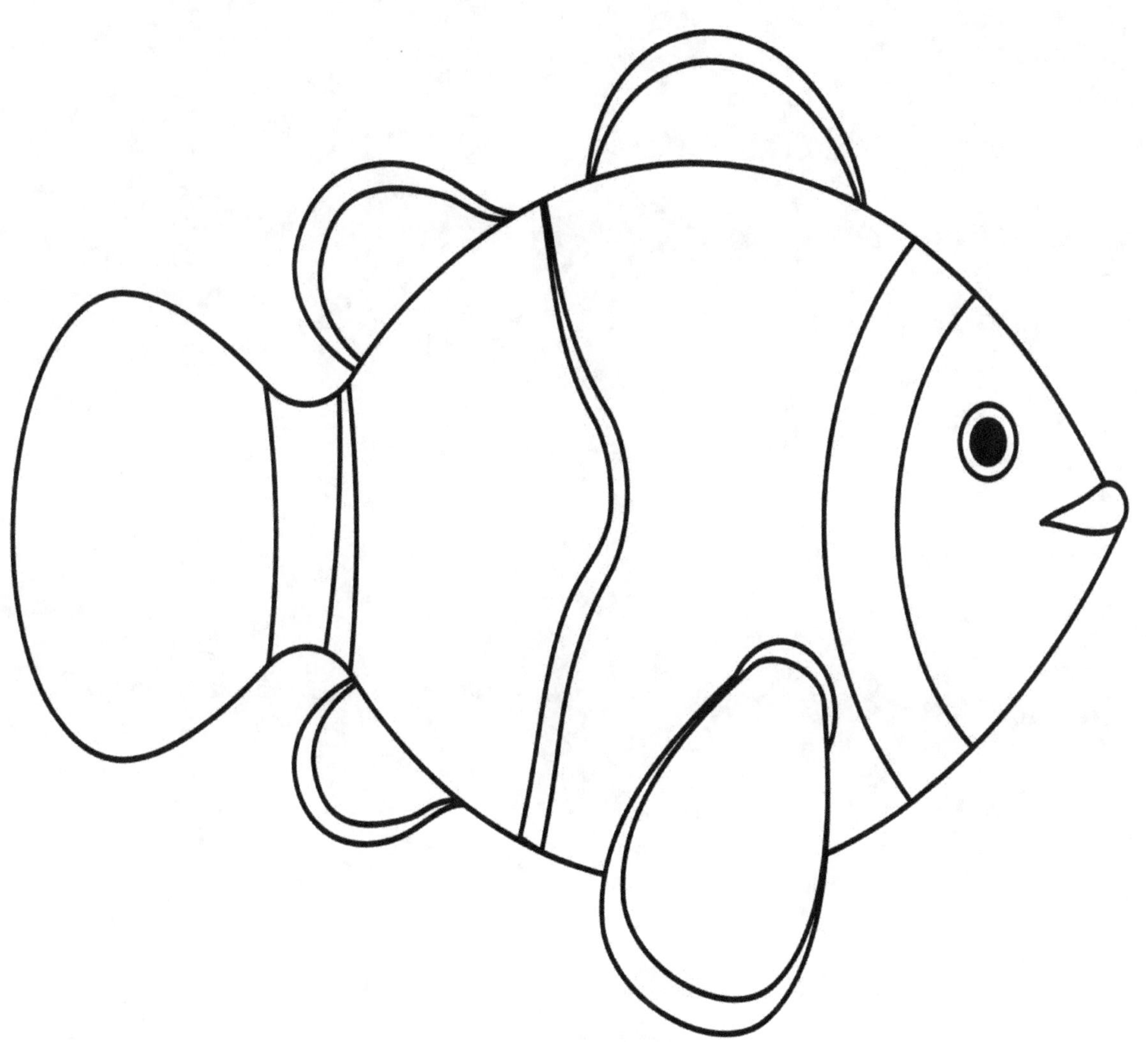

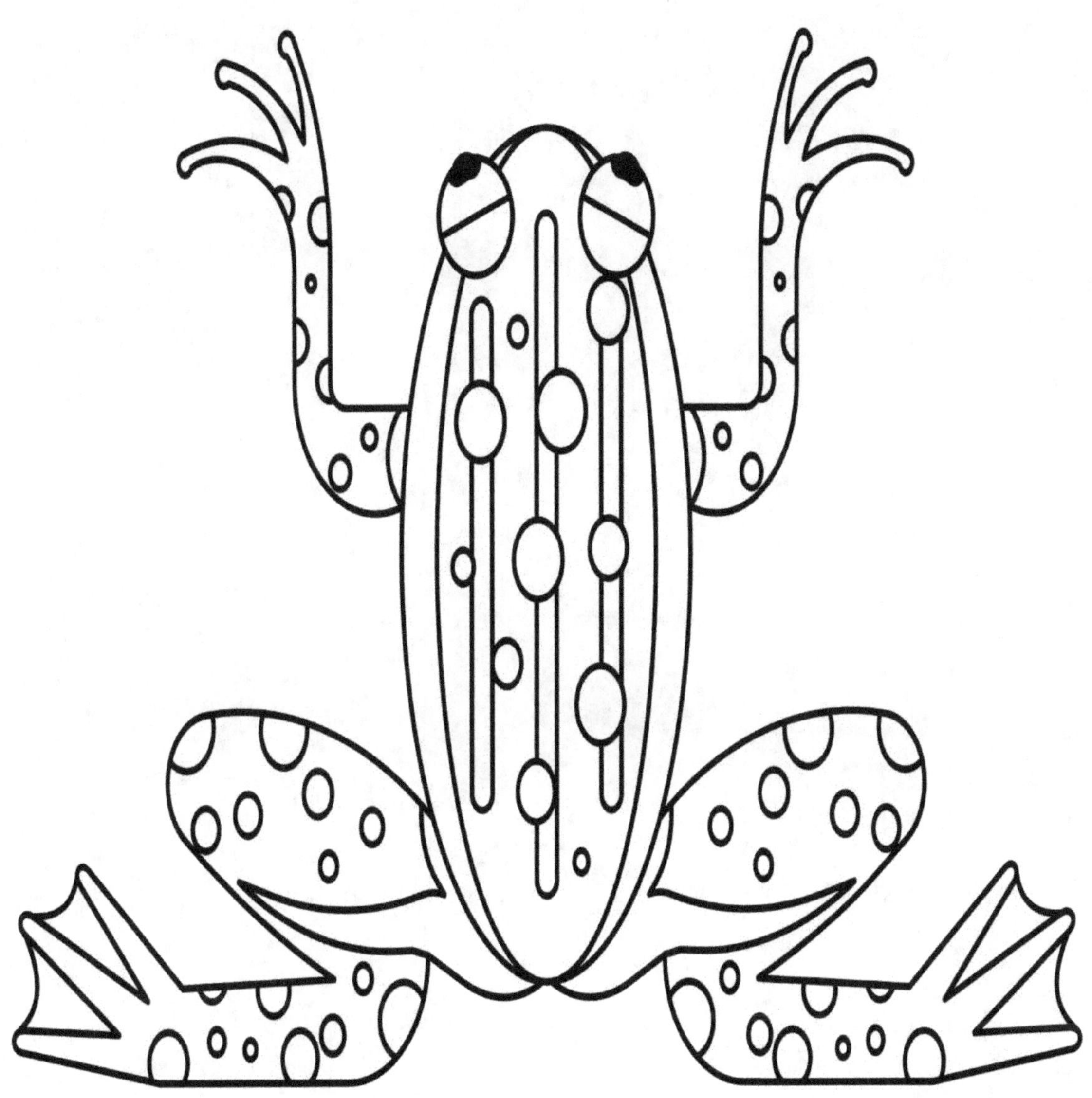

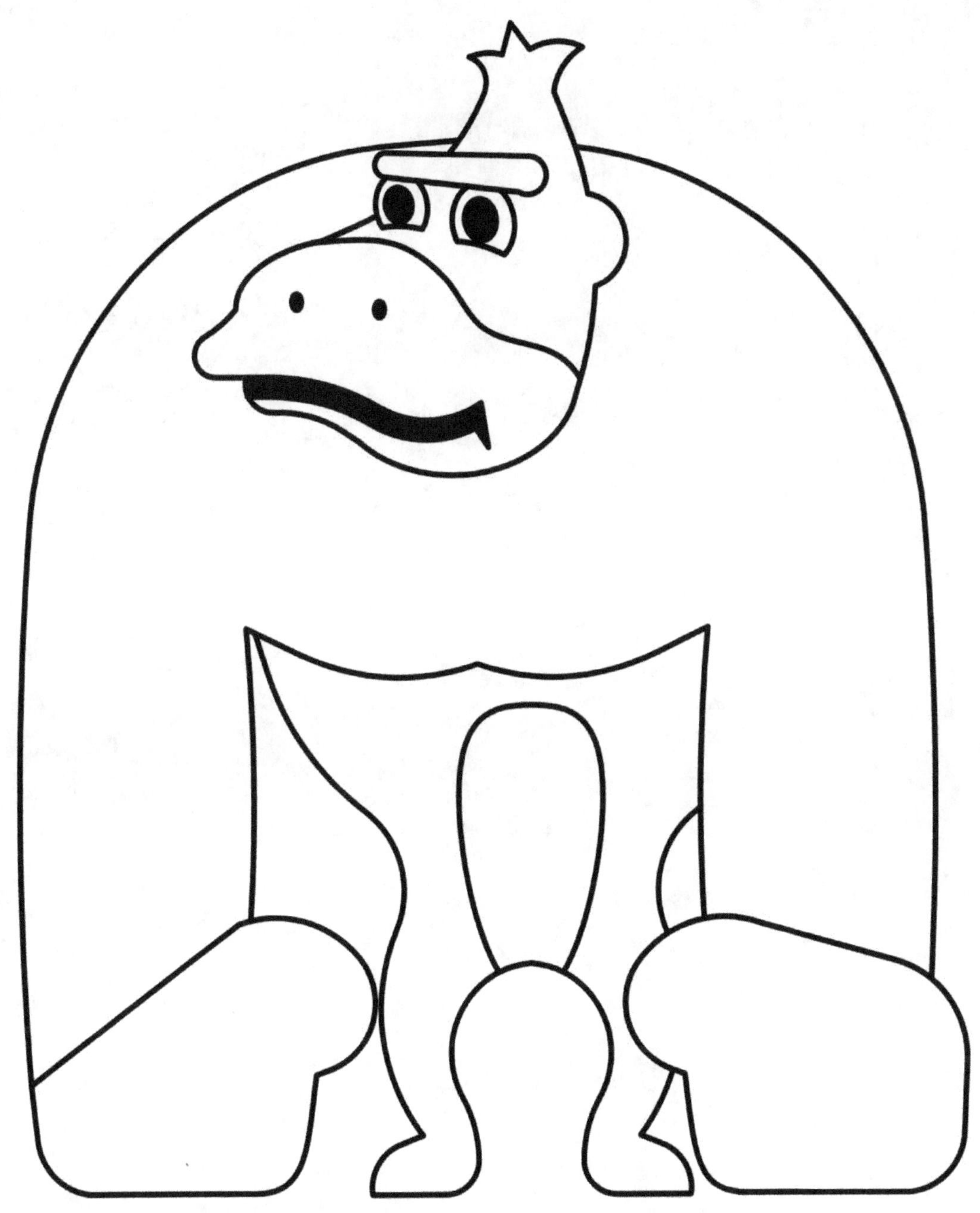

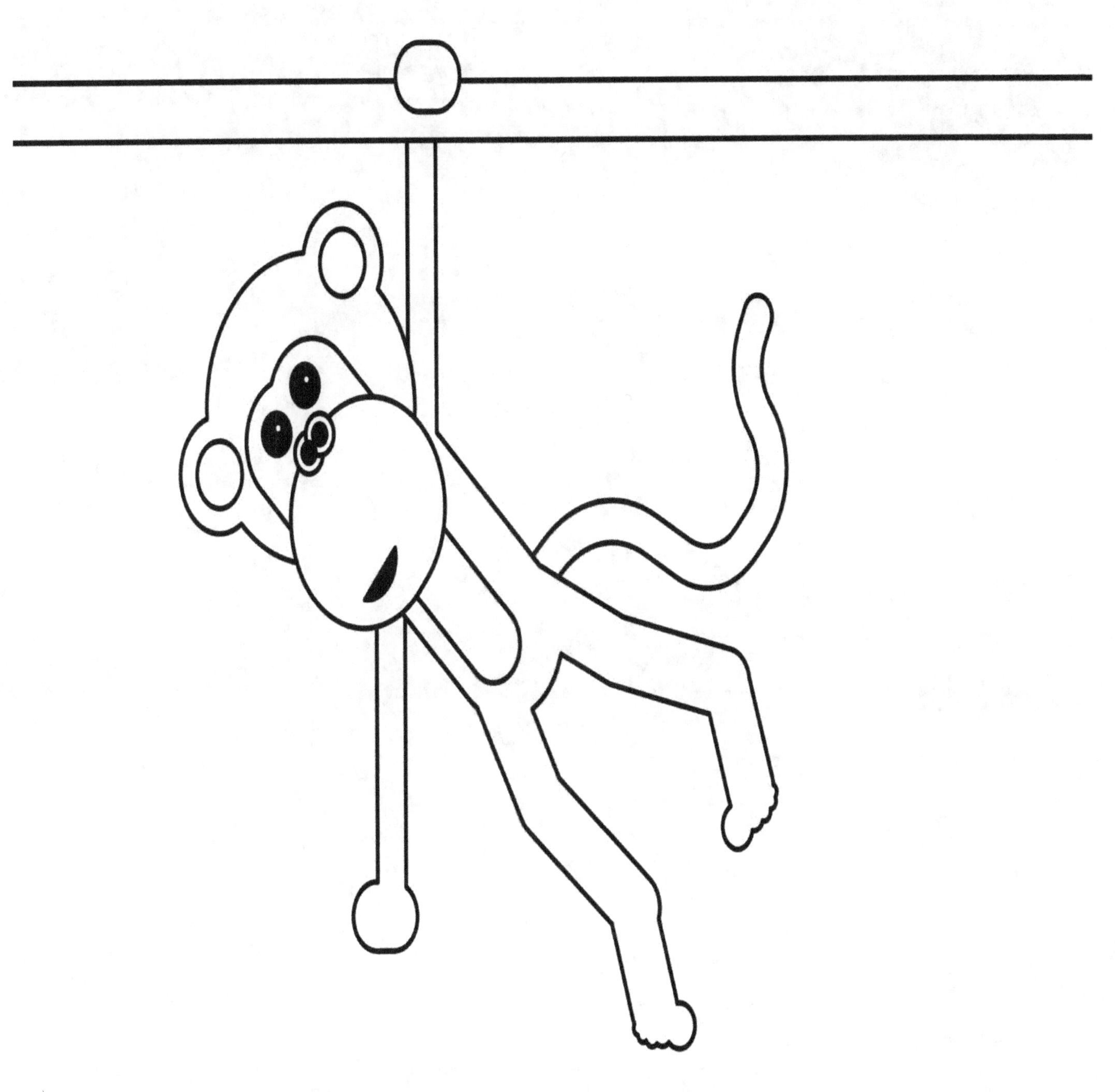

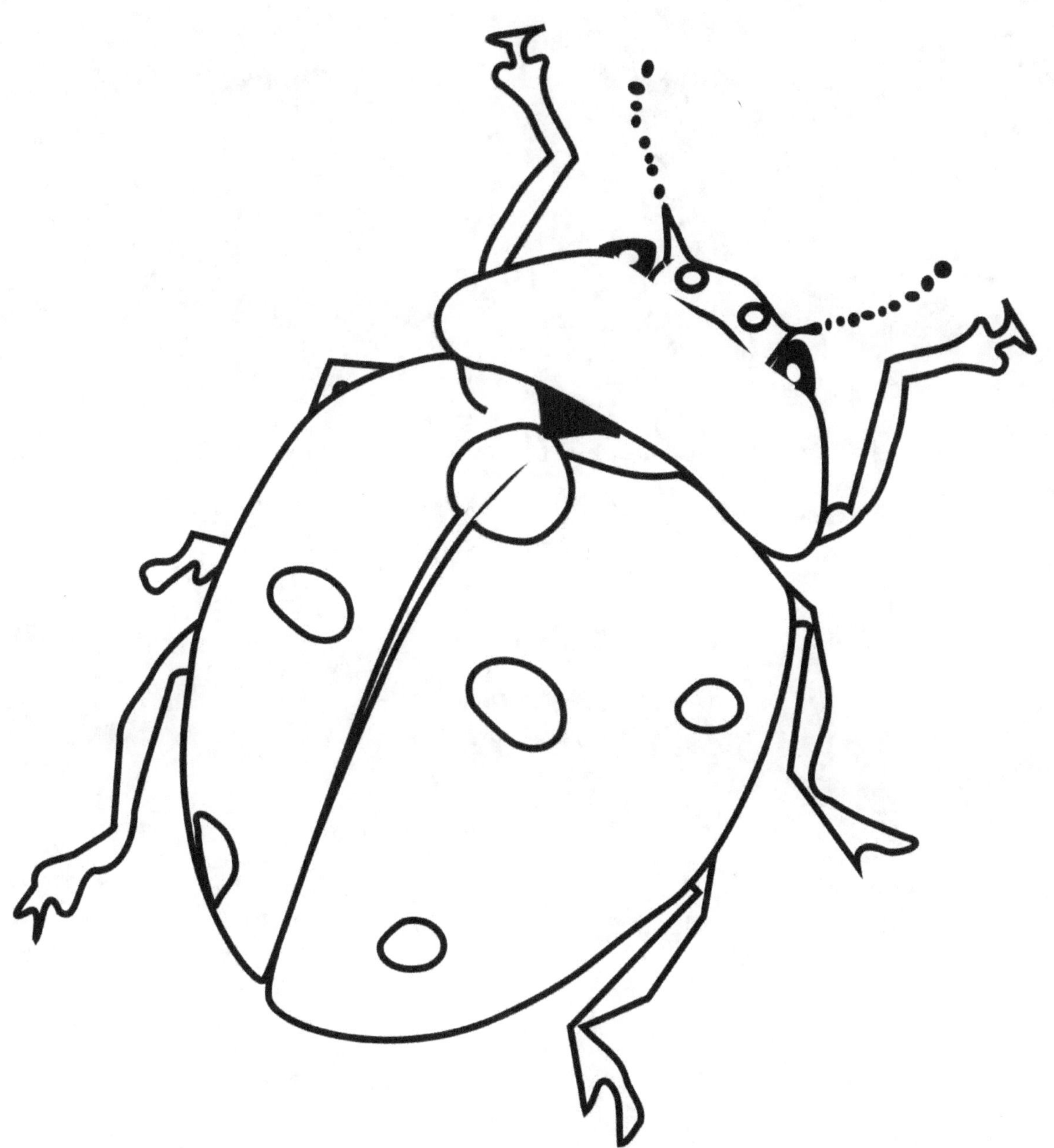

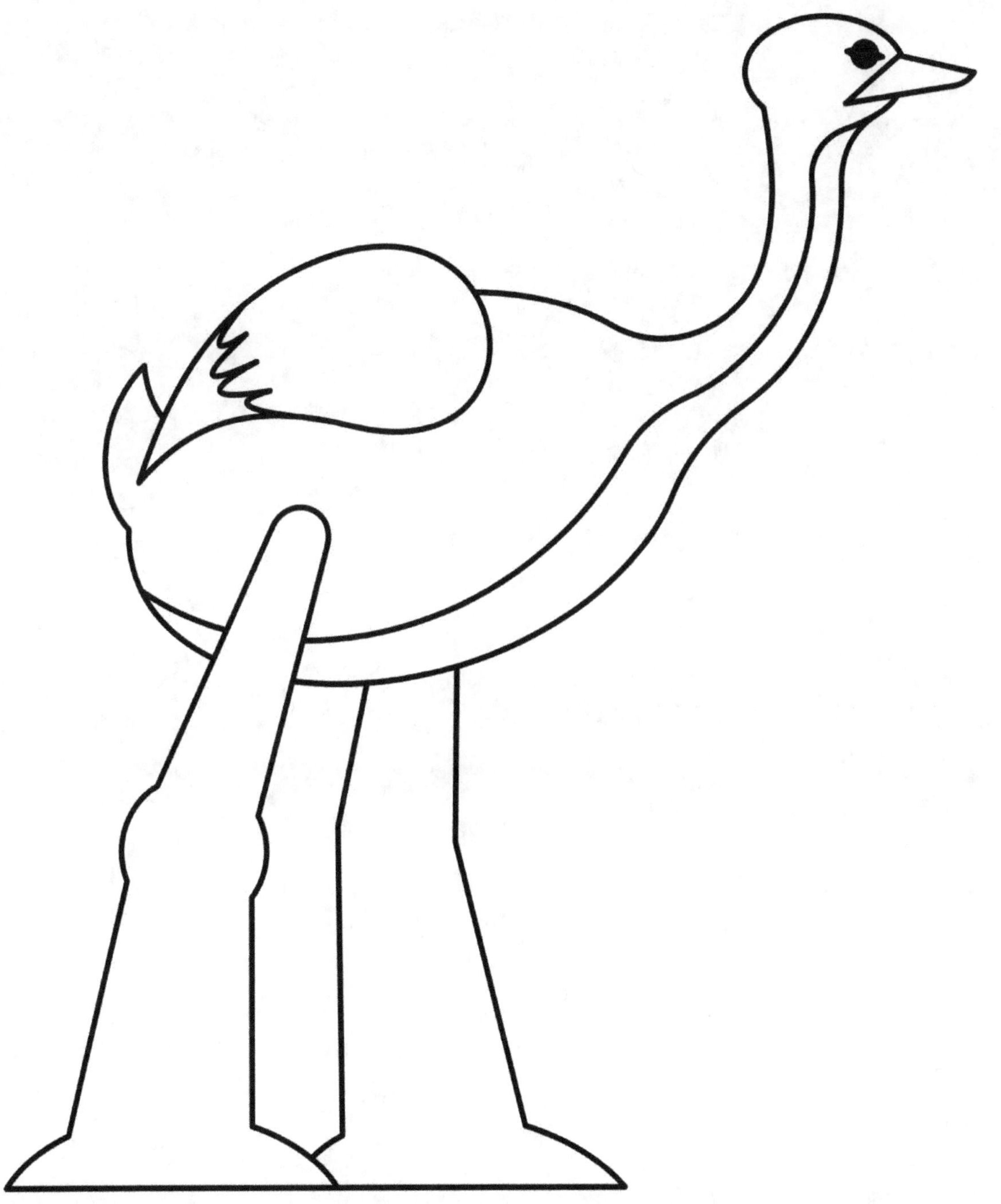

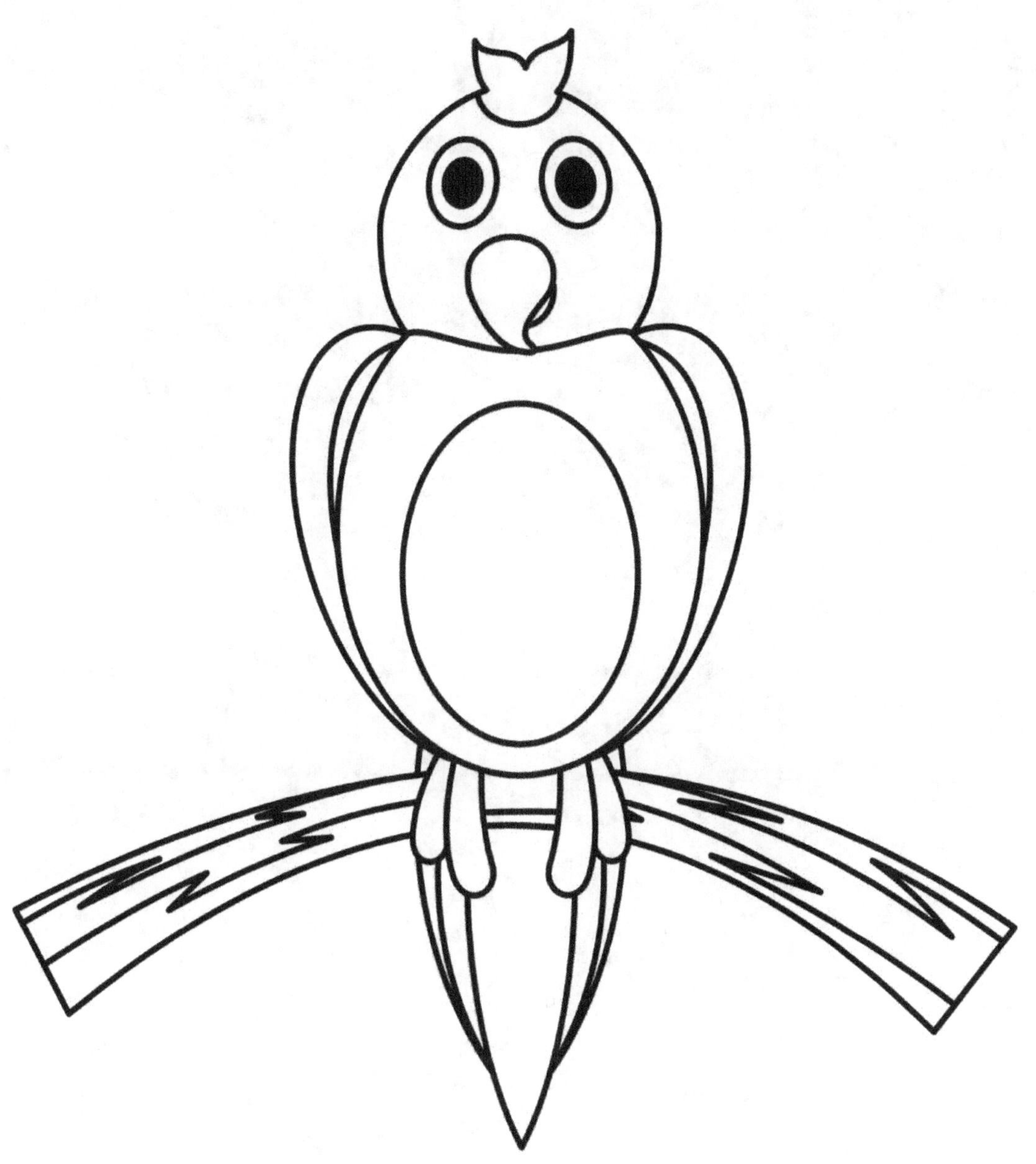

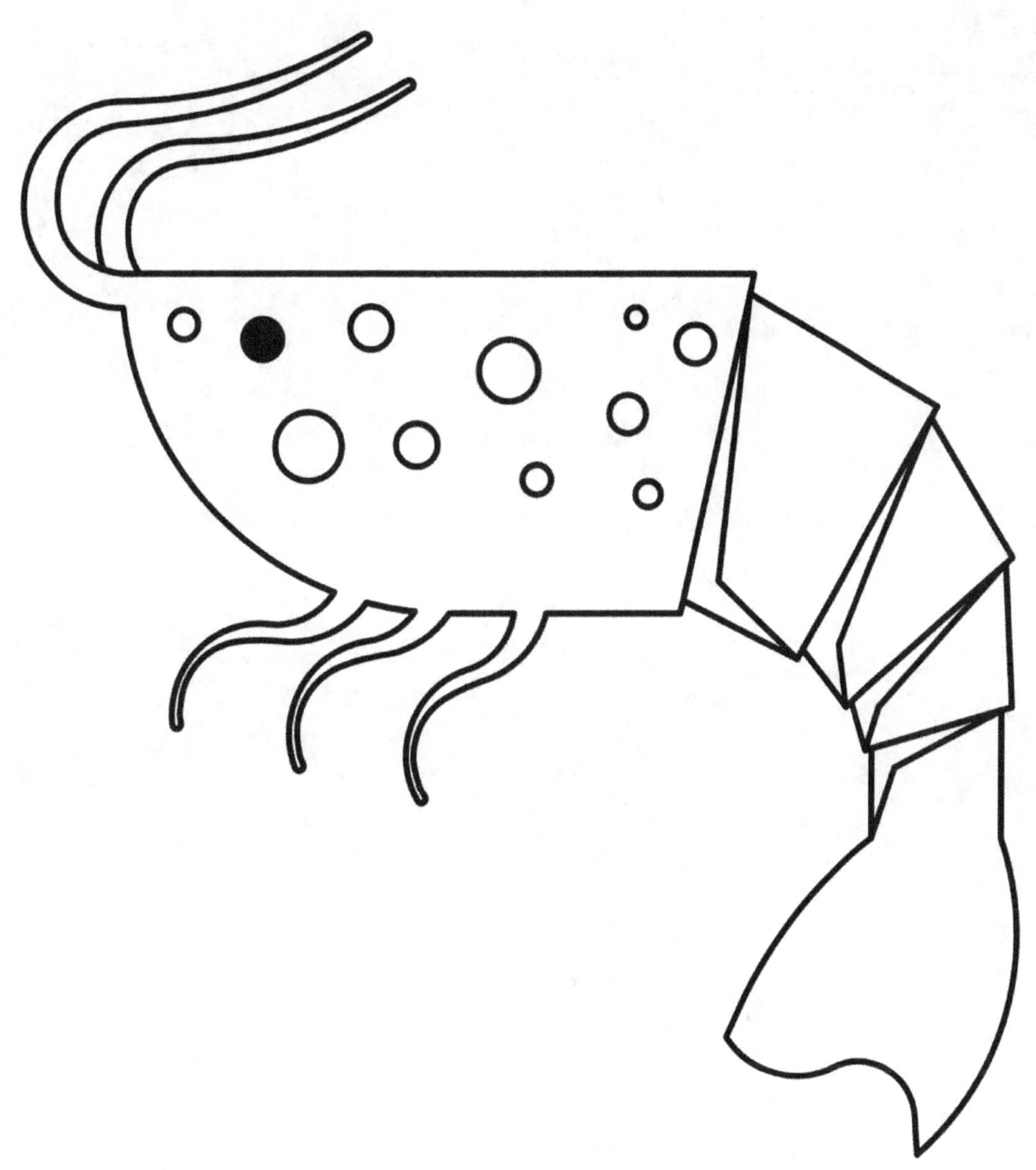

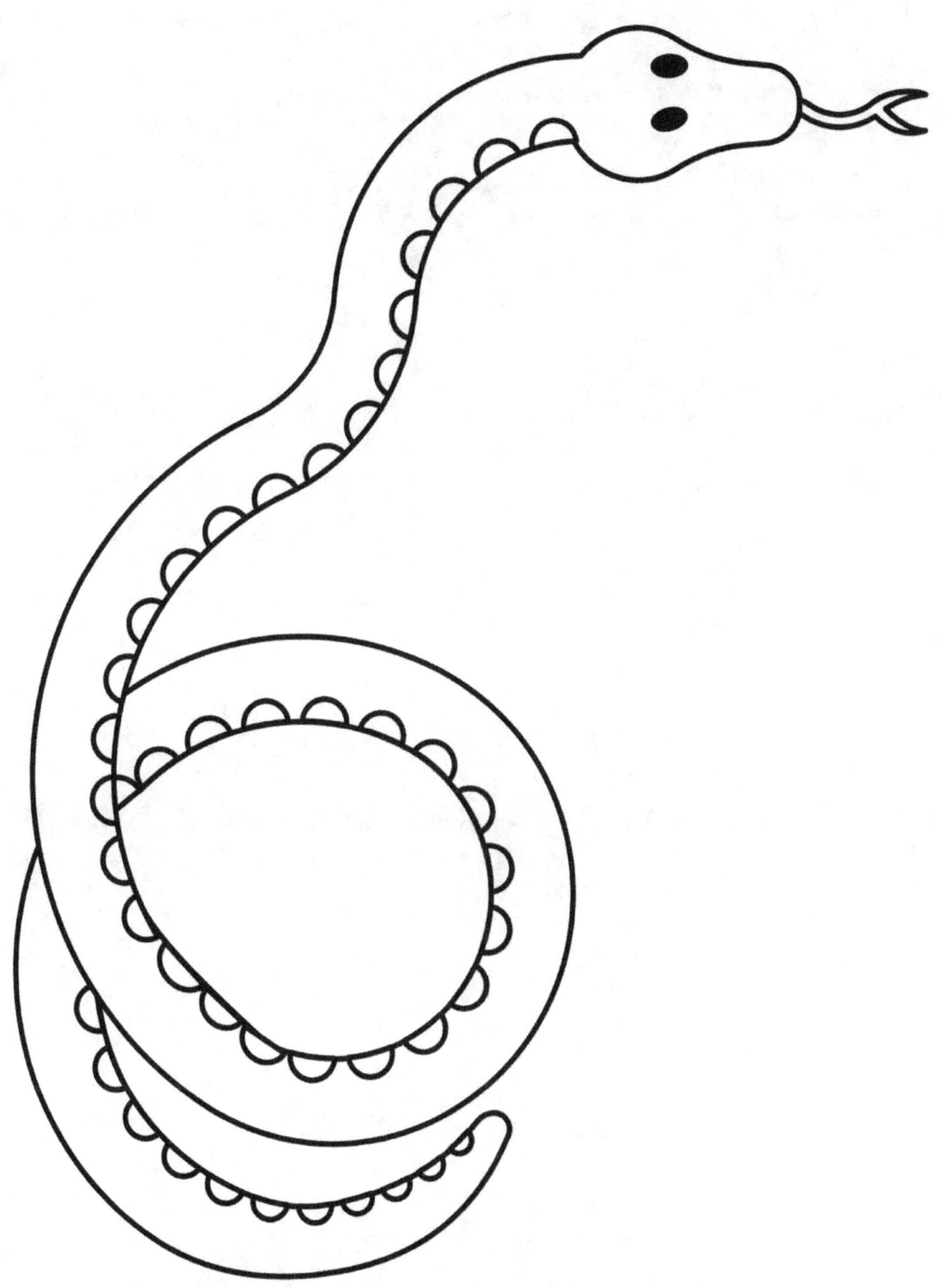

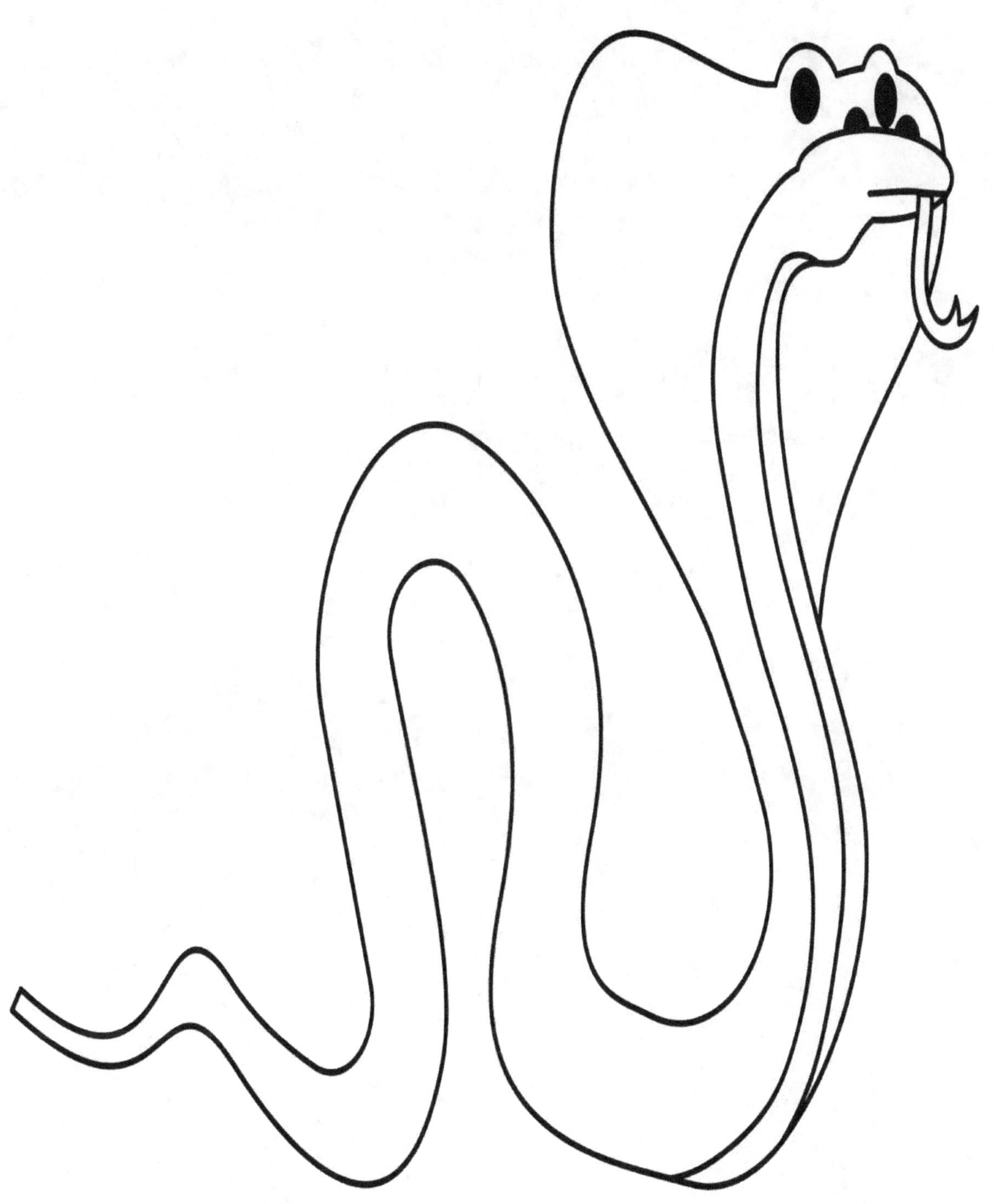

www.ingramcontent.com/pod-product-compliance
Lightning Source LLC
Chambersburg PA
CBHW081416250726
48654CB00013B/1721